A BOOK OF
Friends and Friendship

FOR FRIENDSHIP'S SAKE

For your enjoyment.
Sincere best wishes
Mary Hill

Also by Celia Haddon
published by Michael Joseph

A CHRISTMAS POSY

A LOVER'S POSY

THE LIMITS OF SEX

A MOTHER'S POSY

THE POWERS OF LOVE

GIFTS FROM YOUR GARDEN

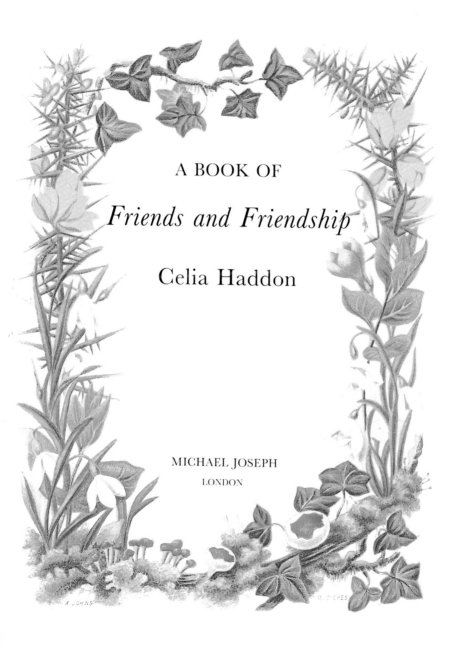

A BOOK OF

Friends and Friendship

Celia Haddon

MICHAEL JOSEPH

LONDON

To Jess

First published in Great Britain by
Michael Joseph Ltd
27 Wrights Lane, London W8 5TZ
1987

British Library Cataloguing in Publication Data
A Book of Friends and Friendship.
1. Friendship—Literary collections
I. Haddon, Celia
808.8'0353   PN6071.F7
ISBN 0-7181-2877-X

Typeset by Cambrian Typesetters, Frimley, Surrey
Printed by Mondadori, Vicenza, Italy

ACKNOWLEDGEMENTS

For permission to reproduce copyright material in this book, the
author and publisher gratefully acknowledge the following:

Erich Fromm, *The Art of Loving*, Unwin Hyman Ltd and Harper
and Row Publishers Inc.;
Kahlil Gibran, *The Prophet*, Random House Inc.;
C. S. Lewis, *The Four Loves*, Fount paperback, Collins;
Konrad Lorenz, *Man Meets Dog*, Methuen and Co.;
A. P. Watt Ltd on behalf of Michael B. Yeats and Macmillan
London Ltd for the use of the poem by W. B. Yeats, which comes
from *The Poems of W. B. Yeats*, edited by Richard Finneran
(Macmillan New York 1983).

CONTENTS

PICTURE CREDITS

page
  8 Frederick Morgan *After School* (Bridgeman Art Library)
 10 Rose M. Barton *Grandad's Garden* (Priory Gallery)
 17 William Collins *Kitten Deceived* (Bridgeman Art Library)
 18 Henry Gillard Glindoni *The Love Letter* (Fine Art Photographic
    Library Ltd)
 23 William Stephen Coleman *At the Stile* (Priory Gallery)
 30 Sir John Pettie *The Shrimpers* (Fine Art Photographic Library
    Ltd)
 34 Paul Seignac *Helping Hands* (Bridgeman Art Library)
 37 Charles E. Wilson *Twixt Sleeping and Waking* (Priory Gallery)
 55 John Gendall *Children Spinning Tops* (Bridgeman Art Library)
 57 Ivan Konstantinovitch Aivazovsky *Farewell to the Black Sea* (Fine
    Art Photographic Library Ltd)
 61 John Morgan *Darby and Joan* (Fine Art Photographic Library
    Ltd)

THE HEART OF FRIENDSHIP

Friends are patient and kind,
they are not jealous or boastful,
they are not arrogant or rude.

Friends do not insist on having their own way,
they are not irritable or resentful,
they do not rejoice at wrong,
but delight in what is right.

Friendship bears all things,
believes all things,
hopes all things,
endures all things.

Friendship
never ends.

Adapted from
Corinthians 1

THE QUALITIES OF A FRIEND

There can be no friendship where there is no freedom.
Friendship loves a free air, and will not be penned up
in straight and narrow enclosures. It will speak freely,
and act so too; and take nothing ill where no ill is
meant; nay, where it is, 'twill easily forgive, and forget
too, upon small acknowledgements.

Friends are true twins in soul; they sympathise in
everything.

One is not happy without the other, nor can either
of them be miserable alone. As if they could change
bodies, they take their turns in pain as well as in
pleasure; relieving one another in their most adverse
conditions.

What one enjoys, the other cannot want. Like the
primitive Christians, they have all things in common,
and no property but in one another.

A true friend unbosoms freely, advises justly, assists
readily, adventures boldly, takes all patiently, defends
courageously, and continues a friend unchangeably.

These being the qualities of a friend, we are to find
them before we choose one.

The covetous, the angry, the proud, the jealous, the
talkative, cannot but make ill friends, as well as the
false.

In short, choose a friend as thou dost a wife, till
death separate you.

WILLIAM PENN 1644–1718

9

A CHOICE OF FRIENDS

That life might be more comfortable yet,
And all my joys refined, sincere and great;
I'd choose two friends, whose company would be
A great advance to my felicity:
Well born, of humours suited to my own,
Discreet, and men, as well as books, have known;
Brave, gen'rous, witty, and exactly free
From loose behaviour, or formality;
Airy, and prudent, merry, but not light,
Quick in discerning, and in judging right.
Secret they should be, faithful to their trust;
In reas'ning cool, strong, temperate and just;
Obliging, open, without huffing brave,
Brisk in gay talking, and in sober, grave;
Close in dispute, but not tenacious, tried
By solid reason, and let that decide;
Not prone to lust, revenge or envious hate,
Nor busy meddlers with intrigues of state;
Strangers to slander, and sworn foes to spite,
Not quarrelsome, but stout enough to fight;
Loyal, and pious, friends to Caesar true,
As dying martyrs to their Maker too;
In their society, I could not miss
A permanent, sincere, substantial bliss.

JOHN POMFRET 1667–1702

11

YOU ARE WHAT YOUR FRIENDS ARE

People will, in a great degree, and not without reason, form their opinion of you, upon that which they have of your friends; and there is a Spanish proverb, which says very justly, 'Tell me whom you live with, and I will tell you who you are.' One may fairly suppose that a man who makes a knave or a fool his friend has something very bad to do, or to conceal. But at the same time that you carefully decline the friendship of knaves and fools, if it can be called friendship, there is no occasion to make either of them your enemies, wantonly, and unprovoked.

The next thing to the choice of your friends is the choice of your company. Endeavour, as much as you can, to keep company with people above you. There you rise, as much as you sink with people below you; for (as I have mentioned before) you are whatever the company you keep is. Do not mistake, when I say company above you, and think that I mean with regard to their birth; that is the least consideration; but I mean with regard to their merit, and the light in which the world considers them.

Every man becomes, to a certain degree, what the people he generally converses with are. He catches their air, their manners, and even their way of thinking. If he observes with attention he will catch them soon; but if he does not, he will at long run contract them insensibly.

LORD CHESTERFIELD 1694–1773

The Tug of War.

FRIENDS – FALSE AND TRUE

If thou wouldest get a friend, prove him first, and be not hasty to credit him.

For some man is a friend for his own occasion, and will not abide in the day of thy trouble.

And there is a friend, who being turned to enmity and strife, will discover thy reproach.

Again, some friend is a companion at the table, and will not continue in the day of thy affliction.

But in thy prosperity he will be as thyself, and will be bold over thy servants.

If thou be brought low, he will be against thee, and will hide himself from thy face.

Separate thyself from thine enemies and take heed of thy friends.

A faithful friend is a strong defence; and he that hath found such an one hath found a treasure.

Nothing doth countervail a faithful friend, and his excellency is invaluable.

A faithful friend is the medicine of life; and they that fear the Lord shall find him.

Whoso feareth the Lord shall direct his friendship aright: for as he is, so shall his neighbour be also.

Ecclesiasticus

Easter Greeting

FALSE FRIENDS-LIKE

When I wer still a bwoy, an' mother's pride,
A bigger bwoy spoke up to me so kind-like,
'If you do like, I'll treat ye wi' a ride
In thease wheel-barrow here.' Zoo I wer blind-like
To what he had a-worken in his mind-like,
An' mounted vor a passenger inside;
An' comen to a puddle, perty wide,
He tipp'd me in, a-grinnen back behind-like.
Zoo when a man do come to me so thick-like,
An' sheake my hand, where woonce he pass'd me by,
An' tell me he would do me this or that,
I can't help thinken o' the big bwoy's trick-like.
An' then, vor all I can but wag my hat
An' thank en, I do veel a little shy.

WILLIAM BARNES, the Dorset poet 1801–86

16

FLATTERY IS NO FRIENDSHIP

Take care thou be not made a fool by flatterers, for even the wisest men are abused by these. Know therefore, that flatterers are the worst kind of traitors; for they will strengthen thy imperfections, encourage thee in all evils, correct thee in nothing, but so shadow and paint all thy vices and follies as thou shalt never, by their will, discern evil from good, or vice from virtue. And because all men are apt to flatter themselves, to entertain the additions of other men's praises is most perilous.

Do not therefore praise thyself, except thou wilt be counted a vainglorious fool, neither take delight in the praises of other men, except thou deserve it, and receive it from such as are worthy and honest, and will withal warn thee of thy faults: for flatterers have never any virtue, they are ever base, creeping, cowardly persons.

It is hard to know them from friends, they are so obsequious and full of protestations; for a wolf resembles a dog, so doth a flatterer a friend. Thou mayest be sure that he that will in private tell thee thy faults is thy friend, for he adventures thy mislike, and doth hazard thy hatred; for there are few men that can endure it, every man for the most part delighting in self-praise, which is one of the most universal follies which bewitcheth mankind.

SIR WALTER RALEIGH 1552–1618

19

THE LOVE UNDERLYING FRIENDSHIP

The most fundamental kind of love, which underlies all types of love, is *brotherly love*. By this I mean the sense of responsibility, care, respect, knowledge of any other human being, the wish to further his life. This is the kind of love the Bible speaks of when it says: love thy neighbour as thyself. Brotherly love is love for all human beings; it is characterised by its very lack of exclusiveness. If I have developed the capacity for love, then I cannot help loving my brothers. In brotherly love there is the experience of union with all men, of human solidarity, of human at-onement. Brotherly love is based on the experience that we are all one. The differences in talents, intelligence, knowledge are negligible in comparison with the identity of the human core common to all men. In order to experience this identity, it is necessary to penetrate from the periphery to the core. If I perceive in another person mainly the surface, I perceive mainly the differences, that which separates us. If I penetrate to the core, I perceive our identity, the fact of our brotherhood . . .

Yet, love of the helpless one, love of the poor and the stranger are the beginnings of brotherly love. To love one's flesh and blood is no achievement. The animal loves its young and cares for them. The helpless one loves his master, since his life depends on him; the child loves his parents, since he needs them. Only in the love of those who do not serve a purpose, love begins to unfold.

ERICH FROMM 1900–80

FRIENDSHIP BETWEEN THE SEXES

It is a wonderful advantage to a man, in every pursuit or avocation, to secure an adviser in a sensible woman. In woman there is at once a subtle delicacy of tact and a plain soundness of judgement, which are rarely combined to an equal degree in man. A woman, if she be really your friend, will have a sensitive regard for your character, honour, repute. She will seldom counsel you to do a shabby thing; for a woman friend desires to be proud of you. At the same time her constitutional timidity makes her more cautious than your male friend. She therefore seldom counsels you to do an imprudent thing. A man's best female friend is a wife of good sense and good heart and who loves him. But supposing the man to be without such a helpmate, female friendship he must have, or his intellect will be without a garden, and there will be many an unheeded gap even in its strongest fence.

Edward Bulwer Lytton 1803–73

FEMALE FRIENDSHIP

Let the dull brutish world that knows not love
Continue heretic, and disapprove
That noble flame; but the refinèd know
'Tis all the Heaven we have here below.
Nature subsists by love, and they do tie
Things to their causes but by sympathy.
Love chains the different elements in one
Great harmony, linked to the heavenly throne.
And as on earth, so the blest quire above
Of saints and angels are maintained by love:
That is their business and felicity,
And will be so, to all eternity.
That is the ocean: our affections here
Are but streams borrowed from the fountain there.
Friendship, like heraldry, is hereby known
Richest when plainest, bravest when alone;
Calm as a virgin, and more innocent
Than sleeping doves are, and as much content
As saints in visions; quiet as the night,
But clear and open as the summer's light;
United more than spirit's faculties;
Higher in thoughts than are the eagle's eyes;
What shall I say? When we two friends are grown,
We're like – Alas, we're like ourselves alone.

KATHERINE PHILIPS 1631–64

FRIENDSHIP WITH ANIMALS

I like cats and dogs very much indeed. They are much superior to human beings as companions. They do not quarrel or argue with you. They never talk about themselves, but listen to you while you talk about yourself, and keep up an appearance of being interested in the conversation. They never say unkind things. They never tell us of our own faults 'merely for our own good'.

They are always glad to see us. They are with us in all our humours. They are merry when we are glad, sober when we feel solemn, sad when we are sorrowful.

And when we bury our face in our hands and wish we had never been born, they don't sit up very straight and observe that we have brought it upon ourselves. They don't even hope it will be a warning to us. But they come up softly; and shove their heads against us. If it is a cat, she stands on your shoulder, rumples your hair, and says 'Lor' I am sorry for you, old man', as plain as words can speak; and if it is a dog, he looks up at you with his big, true eyes, and says with them, 'Well, you've always got me, you know. We'll go through the world together, and always stand by each other won't we?'

He is very imprudent, a dog is. He never makes it his business to inquire whether you are in the right or in the wrong, never bothers as to whether you are going up or down upon life's ladder, never asks whether you are rich or poor, silly or wise, sinner or saint. You are his pal. That is enough for him.

JEROME K. JEROME 1859–1927

A LESSON IN FRIENDSHIP

The greenhouse is my summer seat;
My shrubs displaced from that retreat
Enjoyed the open air;
Two goldfinches, whose sprightly song
Had been their mutual solace long,
Lived happy prisoners there.

They sang, as blithe as finches sing
That flutter loose on golden wing,
And frolic where they list;
Strangers to liberty, 'tis true,
But that delight they never knew,
And, therefore, never missed.

But nature works in every breast;
Instinct is never quite suppressed;
And Dick felt some desires,
Which, after many an effort vain,
Instructed him at length to gain,
A pass between his wires.

The open windows seemed to invite
The freeman to a farewell flight;
But Tom was still confined;
And Dick, although his way was clear,
Was much too gen'rous and sincere
To leave his friend behind.

For, settling on his grated roof,
He chirped and kissed him, giving proof
That he desired no more;
Nor would forsake his cage at last,
Till gently seized I shut him fast,
A prisoner as before.

Oh ye, who never knew the joys
Of Friendship, satisfied with noise,
Fandango, ball and rout!
Blush, when I tell you how a bird
A prison, with a friend, preferred
To liberty without.

WILLIAM COWPER 1731–1800

MAN'S BEST FRIEND

We judge the moral worth of two human friends according to which of them is ready to make the greater sacrifice without thought of recompense. Nietzsche who, unlike most people, wore brutality only as a mask to hide true warmness of heart, said the beautiful words, 'Let it be your aim always to love more than the other, never to be second.' With human beings, I am sometimes able to fulfil this commandment, but in my relations with a faithful dog, I am always the second. What a strange and unique social relationship! Have you ever thought how extraordinary it all is? Man, endowed with reason and a highly developed sense of moral responsibility, whose finest and noblest belief is the religion of brotherly love, in this very respect falls short of the carnivores.

Even today man's heart is still the same as that of the higher social animals, no matter how far the achievements of his reason and his rational moral sense transcend theirs. The plain fact that my dog loves me more than I love him is undeniable and always fills me with a certain feeling of shame.

KONRAD LORENZ 1903–

KEEP FRIENDSHIP IN REPAIR

I have often thought, that as longevity is generally desired, and, I believe, generally expected, it would be wise to be continually adding to the number of our friends, that the loss of some may be supplied by others. Friendship, 'the wine of life', should, like a well-stocked cellar, be thus continually renewed; and it is consolatory to think, that although we can seldom add what will equal the generous first-growths of our youth, yet friendship becomes insensibly old in much less time than is commonly imagined, and not many years are required to make it very mellow and pleasant. Warmth will, no doubt, make a considerable difference. Men of affectionate temper and bright fancy will coalesce a great deal sooner than those who are cold and dull.

Johnson said to Sir Joshua Reynolds, 'If a man does not make new acquaintance as he advances through life, he will soon find himself left alone. A man, Sir, should keep his friendship in *constant repair*.'

JAMES BOSWELL 1740–95

THE COMPOSITION OF FRIENDSHIP

There are two elements that go to the composition of friendship, each so sovereign that I can detect no superiority in either, no reason why either should be first named. One is truth. A friend is a person with whom I may be sincere. Before him I may think aloud. I am arrived at last in the presence of a man so real and equal, that I may drop even those undermost garments of dissimulation, courtesy, and second thought which men never put off, and may deal with him with the simplicity and wholeness with which one chemical atom meets another. Sincerity is the luxury allowed, like diadems and authority, only to the highest rank, *that* being permitted to speak the truth, as having none above it to court or conform unto. Every man alone is sincere. At the entrance of a second person, hypocrisy begins. We parry and fend the approach of our fellow-man by compliments, by gossip, by amusement, by affairs. We cover up our thought from him under a hundred folds.

The other element of friendship is tenderness. We are holden to men by every sort of tie, by blood, by pride, by fear, by hope, by lucre, by lust, by hate, by administration, by every circumstance, and badge and trifle, but we can scarce believe that so much character can subsist in another as to draw us by love. Can another be so blessed, and we so pure, that we can offer him tenderness? When a man becomes dear to me, I have touched the goal of fortune.

RALPH WALDO EMERSON 1803–82

32

FRIENDSHIP BETTER THAN
ROMANTIC LOVE

Friendship is a serious affection; the most sublime of all affections, because it is founded on principle, and cemented by time. The very reverse may be said of love. In a great degree, love and friendship cannot subsist in the same bosom; even when inspired by different objects they weaken or destroy each other, and for the same object can only be felt in succession. The vain fears and fond jealousies, the winds which fan the flame of love, when judiciously or artfully tempered, are both incompatible with the tender confidence and sincere respect of friendship.

MARY WOLLSTONECRAFT 1759–97

THE FALLING OUT OF FAITHFUL FRIENDS

In going to my naked bed, as one that would have slept,
I heard a wife sing to her child, that long before had wept,
She sighèd sore, and sang full sweet to bring the babe to
    rest.
That would not cease; but crièd still, in sucking at her
    breast.
She was full weary of her watch, and grievèd with her child;
She rockèd it and rated it, till that on her it smiled.
Then did she say, 'Now have I found this proverb true to
    prove,
The falling out of faithful friends, renewing is of love.'

Then took I paper, pen, and ink, this proverb for to write,
In register for to remain of such a worthy wight.
As she proceeded thus in song unto her little brat
Much matter uttered she of weight, in place whereas she
    sat:
And provèd plain there was no beast, no creature bearing
    life
Could well be known to live in love, without discord and
    strife.
Then kissèd she her little babe, and sware, by God above,
The falling out of faithful friends, renewing is of love.

RICHARD EDWARDS 1523–66

HOW TO TREAT A FRIEND

Give thy friend counsel wisely and charitably, but leave him to his liberty whether he will follow thee or no: and be not angry if thy counsel be rejected; for 'advice is no empire', and he is not my friend that will be my judge whether I will or no. He that gives advice to his friend and exacts obedience to it, does not the kindness and ingenuity of a friend, but the office and pertness of a school-master.

When you admonish your friend, let it be without bitterness; when you chide him, let it be without reproach; when you praise him, let it be with worthy purposes, and for just causes and in friendly measures; too much of that is flattery, too little is envy; if you do it justly, you teach him true measures: but when others praise him, rejoice, though they praise not thee, and remember that if thou esteemest his praise to be thy disparagement, thou art envious, but neither just nor kind.

After all this, treat thy friend nobly, love to be with him, do to him all the worthinesses of love and fair endearment, according to thy capacity and his; bear with his infirmities till they approach towards being criminal; but never dissemble with him, never despise him, never leave him.

JEREMY TAYLOR 1613–67

FROM FOE TO FRIEND

I wrestle not with rage
While fury's flame doth burn;
It is in vain to stop the stream
Until the tide doth turn.

But when the flame is out,
And ebbing wrath doth end,
I turn a late enlarged foe
Into a quiet friend.

And taught with often proof,
A temper'd calm I find
To be most solace to itself,
Best cure for angry mind.

ROBERT SOUTHWELL 1561-95

THE POISON OF FRIENDSHIP

Alas! they had been friends in youth;
But whispering tongues can poison truth;
And constancy lives in realms above;
And life is thorny; and youth is vain;
And to be wroth with one we love,
Doth work like madness in the brain.
And thus it chanced, as I divine,
With Roland and Sir Leoline.
Each spake words of high disdain
And insult to his heart's best brother:
They parted – ne'er to meet again!
But never either found another
To free the hollow heart from paining –
They stood aloof, the scars remaining,
Like cliffs which had been rent asunder;
A dreary sea now flows between,
But neither heat, nor frost, nor thunder,
Shall wholly do away, I ween,
The marks of that which once hath been.

SAMUEL COLERIDGE 1772–1834

HE

THE HOLLY BOUGH

Ye who have scorned each other,
Or injured friend or brother,
In this fast fading year;
Ye who, by word or deed,
Have made a kind heart bleed,
Come gather here.

Let sinned against and sinning
Forget their strife's beginning,
And join in friendship now;
Be links no longer broken,
Be sweet forgiveness spoken,
Under the Holly Bough.

CHARLES MACKAY 1814–89

LAMENT
FOR HIS FRIEND,
SIR PHILIP SIDNEY

Knowledge his light hath lost, Valor hath slain her knight,
Sidney is dead, dead is my friend, dead is the world's
delight.
Place pensive wails his fall, whose presence was her pride,
Time crieth out: 'My ebb is come, his life was my
springtide.'

Farewell to you my hopes, my wonted waking dreams,
Farewell sometimes enjoyèd joy, eclipsèd are thy beams,
Farewell self-pleasing thoughts, which quietness brings
forth,
And farewell friendship's sacred league, uniting minds of
worth.

And farewell merry heart, the gift of guiltless minds,
And all sports which, for life's restore, variety assigns,
Let all that sweet is, void? In me no mirth may dwell,
Philip, the cause of all this woe, my life's content, farewell.

FULKE GREVILLE 1554–1628

FRIENDS WHO HAVE DIED

They are all gone into the world of light!
And I alone sit lingering here;
Their very memory is fair and bright,
And my sad thoughts doth clear.

I see them walking in an air of glory,
Whose light doth trample on my days:
My days, which are at best but dull and hoary,
Mere glimmering and decays.

Oh holy hope! and high humility,
High as the Heavens above!
These are your walks, and you have shewed them me
To kindle my cold love.

Dear beauteous death! the jewel of the just,
Shining nowhere, but in the dark;
What mysteries do lie beyond thy dust;
Could man outlook that mark!

He that hath found some fledged bird's nest, may know
At first sight, if the bird be flown;
But what fair well, or grove he sings in now,
That is to him unknown.

And yet as angels in some brighter dreams
Call to the soul, when man doth sleep:
So some strange thoughts transcend our wonted themes,
And into glory peep.

If a star were confined into a tomb,
Her captive flames must needs burn there;
But when the hand that locked her up, gives room,
She'll shine through all the sphere.

O Father of eternal life, and all
Created glories under Thee!
Resume Thy spirit from this world of thrall
Into true liberty.

Either disperse these mists, which blot and fill
My perspective (still) as they pass,
Or else remove me hence unto that hill
Where I shall need no glass.

HENRY VAUGHAN 1622–95

In Memoriam.

IN MEMORIAM

Tears of the widower, when he sees
A late-lost form that sleep reveals,
And moves his doubtful arms, and feels
Her place is empty, fall like these;

Which weep a loss for ever new,
A void where heart on heart reposed;
And, where warm hands have prest
    and closed,
Silence, till I be silent too.

Which weep the comrade of my choice,
An awful thought, a life removed,
The human-hearted man I loved,
A Spirit, not a breathing voice.

Come Time, and teach me, many years,
I do not suffer in a dream;
For now so strange do these things seem,
Mine eyes have leisure for their tears;

My fancies time to rise on wing,
And glance about the approaching sails,
As tho' they brought but merchants' bales,
And not the burthen that they bring.

ALFRED TENNYSON 1809–92

Patience

UPHELD BY OUR FRIENDS

With an honest old friend, and a merry old song,
And a flask of old port let me sit the night long,
And laugh at the malice of those who repine,
That they must swig porter, while I can drink wine.

I envy no mortal tho' never so great,
Nor scorn I a wretch for his lowly estate,
But what I abhor, and esteem as a curse,
Is poorness of spirit, not poorness of purse.

Then dare to be generous, dauntless and gay,
Let's merrily pass life's remainder away:
Upheld by our friends, we our foes may despise,
For the more we are envied, the higher we rise.

HENRY CAREY 1687–1743

Cheers for the Navy, and a Happy New Year!

THE FRUITS OF FRIENDSHIP

Little do men perceive, what solitude is, and how far it extendeth. For a crowd is not company; and faces are but a gallery of pictures; and talk but a tinkling cymbal, where there is no love. But we may go further, and affirm most truly: that it is a mere, and miserable solitude to want true friends; without which the world is but a wilderness.

The principal fruit of friendship is the ease and discharge of the fullness and swellings of the heart, which passions of all kinds do cause and induce. We know diseases of stoppings and suffocations are the most dangerous in the body; and it is not much otherwise in the mind. No receipt openeth the heart, but a true friend; to whom you may impart griefs, joys, fears, hopes, suspicions, counsels, and whatsoever lieth upon the heart, to oppress it, in a kind of civil shrift or confession.

The second fruit of friendship is healthful and sovereign for the understanding, as the first is for the affections. For friendship maketh indeed a fair day in the affections from storm and tempests: but it maketh daylight in the understanding, out of darkness and confusion of thoughts. Neither is this to be understood only of faithful counsel, which a man receiveth from his friend; but before you come to that, certain it is, that whosoever hath his mind fraught with many thoughts, his wits and understanding do clarify and break up in the communicating and discoursing with another: he tosseth his thoughts more easily; he marshalleth them more orderly; he seeth how they look when they are turned into words.

Add now, to make this second fruit of friendship

complete, that other point, which lieth more open and falleth within vulgar observation; which is faithful counsel from a friend. There is as much difference between the counsel that a friend giveth, and that a man giveth himself, as there is between the counsel of a friend and of a flatterer. For there is no such flatterer as is a man's self; and there is no such remedy against flattery of a man's self, as the liberty of a friend.

After these two noble fruits of friendship (peace in the affections and support of the judgement) followeth the last fruit, which is like the pomegranite full of many kernels; I mean aid and bearing a part in all actions and occasions. Here the best way to represent to life the manifold use of friendship is to cast and see how many things there are which a man cannot do himself. Men have their time and die many times in desire of some things, which they principally take to heart; the bestowing of a child, the finishing of a work, or the like. If a man have a true friend, he may rest almost secure, that the care of those things will continue after him.

FRANCIS BACON 1560–1626

FRIENDSHIP IS A REBELLION

Every real Friendship is a sort of secession, even a rebellion. It may be a rebellion of serious thinkers against accepted clap-trap or of faddists against accepted good sense; of real artists against popular ugliness or of charlatans against civilised taste; of good men against the badness of society or of bad men against its goodness. Whichever it is, it will be unwelcome to Top People. In each knot of Friends there is a sectional 'public opinion' which fortifies its members against the public opinion of the community in general. Each therefore is a pocket of potential resistance. Men who have real Friends are less easy to manage or 'get at'; harder for good Authorities to correct or for bad Authorities to corrupt. Hence if our masters, by force or by propaganda about 'Togetherness' or by unobtrusively making privacy and unplanned leisure impossible, ever succeed in producing a world where all are Companions and none are Friends, they will have removed certain dangers, and will also have taken from us what is almost our strongest safeguard against complete servitude.

C. S. LEWIS 1898–1963

THE PROPHET DESCRIBES FRIENDSHIP

Your friend is your needs answered.

He is your field which you sow with love and reap with thanksgiving.

And he is your board and your fireside.

For you come to him with your hunger, and you seek him for peace.

When your friend speaks his mind you fear not the 'nay' in your own
    mind, nor do you withhold the 'ay'.

And when he is silent your heart ceases not to listen to his heart;

For without words, in friendship, all thoughts, all desires, all
    expectations are born and shared, with joy that is unacclaimed.

When you part from your friend, you grieve not;

For that which you love most in him may be clearer in his absence, as
    the mountain to the climber is clearer from the plain.

And let there be no purpose in friendship save the deepening of the
    spirit.

For love that seeks aught but the disclosure of its own mystery is not
    love but a net cast forth: and only the unprofitable is caught.

And let your best be for your friend.

If he must know the ebb of your tide, let him know its flood also.

For what is your friend that you should seek him with hours to kill?

Seek him always with hours to live.

For it is his to fill your need, but not your emptiness.

And in the sweetness of friendship let there be laughter, and sharing of
    pleasures.

For in the dew of little things the heart finds its morning and is
    refreshed.

KAHLIL GIBRAN 1883–1931

CHEERING ADVICE TO A FRIEND

1st. Live as well as you dare.

2nd. Go into the shower-bath with a small quantity of water at a temperature low enough to give you a slight sensation of cold, 75° or 80°.

3rd. Amusing books.

4th. Short views of human life – not further than dinner or tea.

5th. Be as busy as you can.

6th. See as much as you can of those friends who respect and like you.

7th. And of those acquaintances who amuse you.

8th. Make no secret of low spirits to your friends, but talk of them freely – they are always worse for dignified concealment.

9th. Attend to the effects tea and coffee produce upon you.

10th. Compare your lot with that of other people.

11th. Don't expect too much from human life – a sorry business at the best.

12th. Avoid poetry, dramatic representations (except comedy), music, serious novels, melancholy sentimental people, and everything likely to excite feeling or emotion not ending in active benevolence.

13th. *Do good*, and endeavour to please everybody of every degree.

14th. Be as much as you can in the open air without fatigue.

15th. Make the room where you commonly sit gay and pleasant.

16th. Struggle by little and little against idleness.

17th. Don't be too severe upon yourself, or underrate yourself, but do yourself justice.

18th. Keep good blazing fires.

19th. Be firm and constant in the exercise of rational religion.

SYDNEY SMITH 1771–1845

The Bird in yonder cage confined,
Sings but to Lovers fond, sincere.

On wings of faith and hope, combined,
Brings soft emotion fondly dear.

SIDE BY SIDE

Don't walk in front of me,
I may not follow.
Don't walk behind me,
I may not lead.
Walk beside me,
And just be my friend.

AUTHOR UNKNOWN

THE LOVER PLEADS WITH HIS FRIEND
FOR OLD FRIENDS

Though you are in your shining days,
Voices among the crowd
And new friends busy with your praise,
Be not unkind or proud,
But think about old friends the most:
Time's bitter flood will rise,
Your beauty perish and be lost
For all eyes but these eyes.

W. B. YEATS 1865–1939

AULD LANG SYNE

Should auld acquaintance be forgot,
And never brought to min'?
Should auld acquaintance be forgot,
And auld lang syne?

> For auld lang syne, my dear.
> For auld lang syne,
> We'll tak a cup o' kindness yet,
> For auld lang syne.

We twa have paidled i' the burn,
From morning sun till dine;
But seas between us braid hae roar'd
Sin' auld lang syne.

And here's a hand, my trusty fiere,
And gie's a hand o' thine;
And we'll tak a right guid-willie waught,
For auld lang syne.

And surely ye'll be your pint-stowp,
And surely I'll be mine;
And we'll tak a cup o' kindness yet
For auld lang syne.

ROBERT BURNS 1759–96

For
Old
Acquaintance

A PRAYER FOR
OUR FRIENDS

O blessed Lord, who hast
commanded us to love one
another, grant us grace that
having received thine
undeserved bounty,
we may love
everyone in thee and for thee.
We implore thy clemency
for all; but especially for
the friends whom
thy love has given to us.
Love thou them, –
O thou fountain of love,
and make them to love thee
with all their heart, that they
may will, and speak, and
do those things only
which are pleasing
to thee.

St Anselm 1033–1109